Never A Good Girl

The Renegade Spirit
of the Farrell-Wilson Family

Never A Good Girl

The Renegade Spirit
of the Farrell-Wilson Family

Hillary Kidd

Jessica Bell

THE
DONNING COMPANY
PUBLISHERS

The Donning Company Publishers
184 Business Park Drive, Suite 206
Virginia Beach, VA 23462

Steve Mull, General Manager
Barbara Buchanan, Office Manager
Pamela Koch, Senior Editor
Kathy Adams, Graphic Designer/Imaging Artist
Tonya Washam, Research and Marketing Supervisor
Pamela Engelhard, Marketing Coordinator
Kathy Snowden Railey, Project Research Coordinator

Jim Railey, Project Director

Library of Congress Cataloging-in-Publication Data

Kidd, Hillary, 1980–
    Never a good girl : the renegade spirit of the Farrell-Wilson Family / by Hillary Kidd and Jessica Bell.
        pages cm
    Includes bibliographical references.
    ISBN 978-1-57864-809-2 (soft cover : alkaline paper)
1. Farrell, Mary Alice, 1859–1934. 2. Wilson, Ammie, 1880–1972. 3. Farrell, Mary Alice—Family. 4. Plano (Tex.)—Biography. 5. Women—Texas—Plano—Biography. 6. Women farmers—Texas—Plano—Biography. 7. Farm life—Texas—Plano—History. 8. Plano (Tex.)—Social life and customs. 9. Heritage Farmstead Museum (Plano, Tex.)—History. I. Bell, Jessica, 1984– II. Title.
    F394.P62K53 2013
    976.4'556060922–dc23
    [B]
                                    2012049225

Printed in the United States of America at Walsworth Publishing Company

Table of Contents

Acknowledgments

This book has been an absolute joy to work on, and I am honored to share the amazing lives of Mary Alice Farrell and Ammie Wilson with the public. I would like to thank my colleagues, board of trustees, and volunteers at the Heritage Farmstead Museum for their unwavering support for this project. All photos not otherwise credited are from the Ammie Wilson Collection at the Heritage Farmstead Museum. This book would not have come together without the generous assistance from Joan Biggerstaff, Nel Byrd, the Carpenter family, Frank and Mary DePeri, Tom Dwyer, Carmen Haggard and the Haggard family, Marie Humphrey, Lloyd Kerr, Lolisa Laenger, Gordon McCosh and family, Peggy and Dorothy Mitchell, Dr. Monte Monroe and the Southwest Collection Special Collections Library at Texas Tech University, Bill and Kathy Pritchett, the Raiden family, Senator Florence Shapiro, Hal Simon, Cheryl Smith and the Plano Library System, Page and Caryetta Thomas, and Candace Morrison Volz. Thank you to Kathy Adams, Pamela Engelhard, Pamela Koch, and Jim Railey of Donning Company Publishers and to the Collin County Historical Commission for their generous grant, which was the catalyst for bringing this story to life. Finally, thank you to my family and friends for their encouragement and to Jessica Bell, my co-author, for her tireless help with the research and writing.

Hillary Kidd
Curator of Collections and Exhibitions
Heritage Farmstead Museum

I would like to thank my family and friends for their encouragement while working on this project. Thank you to all of the staff at the Heritage Farmstead Museum for their help, to Marcia Britton, my advisor at the University of Oklahoma, for her guidance at the beginning stages of writing, and finally I would also like to thank my co-author, Hillary Kidd.

Jessica Bell
Curatorial Researcher
Heritage Farmstead Museum

Family Tree

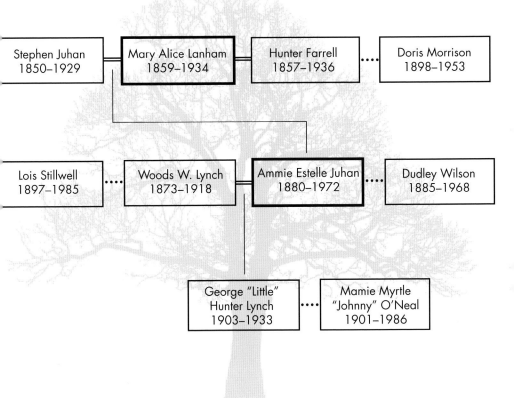

| Stephen Juhan 1850–1929 | Mary Alice Lanham 1859–1934 | Hunter Farrell 1857–1936 | Doris Morrison 1898–1953 |

| Lois Stillwell 1897–1985 | Woods W. Lynch 1873–1918 | Ammie Estelle Juhan 1880–1972 | Dudley Wilson 1885–1968 |

| George "Little" Hunter Lynch 1903–1933 | Mamie Myrtle "Johnny" O'Neal 1901–1986 |

•••• Marriage

═══ Divorce

Hunter Thomas Farrell, circa 1885

A low murmur among the audience arose as the judge called Hunter Farrell to the stand. A handsome young man stood and glanced around the room. A slight smirk spread across his tanned face. His strong features and twill suit gave him a distinguished look on that cold February morning in 1889. As others struggled with the chill of the courtroom, Hunter strolled briskly to the stand. As the attention shifted to the judge who prepared to speak, no one seemed to notice the discerning glance between the plaintiff in the divorce proceedings, Mary Alice Lanham Juhan, and the witness her lawyer had just called to testify on her behalf.

Judge Robert Burke peered over his thick, walrus mustache and calmly ordered the proceedings to continue. "Mr. Farrell," began Mr. McCoy, the attorney for Mary Alice, "Will you please describe the circumstances you witnessed between Mary Alice and Stephen Juhan?" "Why yes sir," the captivating man continued, "Juhan was quite abusive in his actions towards poor Mrs. Juhan."

As the morning progressed, Farrell compelled listeners with his sincere manner of speaking and accounts of the physical and mental abuses by Juhan toward his wife. By the end of the proceedings, one week later, Mary Alice Juhan was not only granted a divorce but also gained full custody of her nine-year-old daughter, Ammie Estelle.

One week after the final divorce decree, Mary Alice entered another courthouse, this time in Collin County. Her young daughter accompanied her, and they were both wearing their Sunday finest. For this courthouse appearance, she seemed more nervous than before, as she ran her hands over her tightly wound bun. "You look striking," a familiar voice echoed from behind. As Mary Alice turned, she saw that Hunter Farrell had come into the hallway.

He took her hand, and the hand of her young daughter, and led them into the County Clerk's office. This time, there was no judge or room full of onlookers, just a clerk bearing witness as Mary Alice Lanham Juhan became Mary Alice Farrell.

Mary Alice Lanham Juhan Farrell, circa 1910

Mary Alice Lanham Juhan Farrell, circa 1910

A Town Called Plano

"You may all go to Hell, and I'll go to Texas."

Davy Crockett uttered these famous words in 1835, prompting a settlement drive to the Republic of Texas. In North Texas a land grant incentive, named Peters Colony, was underway, allotting settlers free tracks of land or head rights. The first settlers came to the Collin County area in early 1841, and the development of the town of Plano began when William Forman, along with his family from Nelson County, Kentucky, purchased the head rights of Sanford Beck in 1846. By 1851, Forman had opened a general store and post office, establishing the focal point of the community. Growth temporarily halted during the Civil War; however, with the completion of the Houston and Texas Railroad in 1872, population boomed, and the town was platted and incorporated in 1873.

During the late nineteenth century, there were a few minor setbacks in the progression of the town when two devastating fires ripped through the heart of Plano. The first fire, in 1881, burned the city's wooden buildings, destroying more than fifty businesses and forcing reconstruction using primarily brick. However, by 1888, Plano had bounced back as a "retail outlet" for farmers on the Blackland Prairie. In 1882, the first school, The Plano Institute,

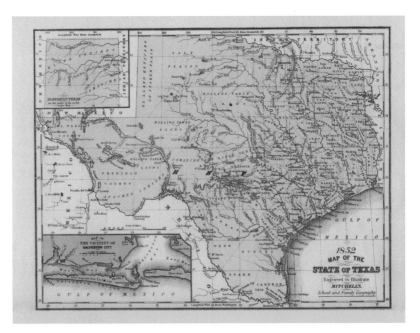

1852 map of Texas.

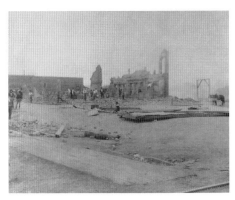

1895 Plano fire. Courtesy of the Frances Bates Wells Collection, Plano Public Library.

opened and was later incorporated into the public school system in 1891. Four years later, in 1895, a second large-scale fire spread through the city. In all, the fire destroyed fifty-one businesses and burned a large portion of Mechanic Street.

Throughout the beginning of the twentieth century, the population of the small farming community increased steadily, with the years following World War II showing remarkable growth. In 1960, Plano had fewer than four thousand people and by 1970, the population had quadrupled to more than seventeen thousand residents. The early 1980s were years of phenomenal growth for the thriving community. Corporate

Plano High School, 1898. Courtesy of Frances Bates Wells Collection, Plano Public Library.

Carlisle Grocery, circa 1900. Hunter Farrell in left foreground. Courtesy of Frances Bates Wells Collection, Plano Public Library.

1891 map of Plano, Texas. Courtesy of the Frances Bates Wells Collection, Plano Public Library.

industries, such as EDS and Frito-Lay, contributed to a steady work environment, with home prices remaining stable even after the economic downturn of the mid-1970s. Throughout the 1980s and 1990s, Plano continued to boom with industry and population growth, and by 2010 the population had reached approximately 260,000 residents, with several major corporations calling Plano their home.

Schimelpfenig Store, circa 1895. Courtesy of the Frances Bates Wells Collection, Plano Public Library.

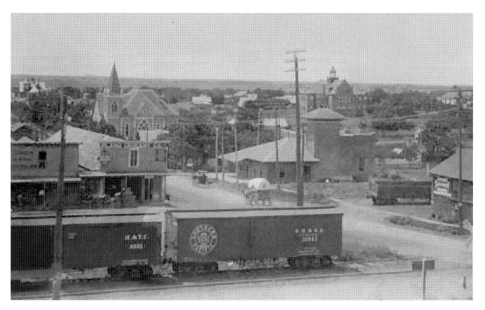

Downtown Plano, circa 1902. Courtesy of the Plano Public Library.

Ammie Lynch sent this postcard of downtown Plano, Texas, to her mother-in-law, Colistia Lynch, in 1907.

A House Divided: Hunter and Mary Alice Farrell

Mary Alice Lanham
Juhan Farrell

Hunter Thomas Farrell

Before the fateful meeting and subsequent marriage to Hunter Farrell, Mary Alice Lanham had grown up as a small-town Texas girl. She was born in Collin County, Texas, to Able and Elisa Lanham on November 18, 1859. Little is known of Mary Alice's life before she married Stephen O. Juhan on September 11, 1879; however, on June 24, 1880, the couple was blessed with a daughter, Ammie Estelle.

Four years before the beginning of the Civil War, Hunter Thomas Farrell was born on November 15, 1857, to Joel and Mary Farrell of Roanoke, Virginia. Hunter would spend most of his adolescence surrounded by conflict, first during the Civil War, then during Reconstruction. Searching for a better life, the Farrell family migrated to the Plano, Texas, area during the 1870s. Hunter quickly made his name in the community in a multitude of ways. He was a highly regarded businessman and farmer. However, his personal life earned him the reputation of being a popular bachelor with a "colorful character," and his exploits provided for frequent acknowledgment in the local newspapers.

In January 1887 he appeared in the *Dallas Morning News* for a brawl; however, he was better known within the community as a ladies' man. In April of that same year, he again graced the newspapers; this time the charges were more severe. Farrell was the catalyst in a tragic confrontation between Charles Henry and his wife, Ellen.

An affair between Farrell and Ellen Henry began sometime in 1886 while the Henry family was living in Plano. According to newspaper reports, Farrell started taking Mrs. Henry to church and soon thereafter began regularly visiting her home while Mr. Henry was at work. Not long after the affair began, Mrs. Henry

PLANO PICKUPS.

Death of an Estimable Young Man—Brother in-Law Fight—A Slugging Match.

PLANO, Jan. 4.—Charley McKarny, an estimable young man about 23 years old died of typhoid fever last night. H numerous friends here sincerely regret h untimely death.

Charley Sandifer and Will Campbell, h brother-in-law, engaged in a fight here ye terday, in which Sandifer severely be Campbell over the head with an axe handl cutting several ugly gashes, which had be sewed up. The cause of the fight wa Sandifer's wife informed him that Cam bell, her brother, had slapped her, an Sandifer chastised him in the manner stat above. They were both arrested and co tributed to the city's fund.

Yesterday evening Will Pearce an Hunter Farrell fought a few rounds an made the claret flow freely, when they we separated by friends.

This *Dallas Morning News* article from January 5, 1887, describes a brawl involving Hunter Farrell. Courtesy of the *Dallas Morning News.*

A TERRIBLE TRAGEDY.

Charles Henry Shoots His Wife for Alleged Inconstancy — The Statement of Mr. Henry.

About 3 p. m. yesterday Charles Henry, a mechanical engineer in the employ of Boyd & Webster. shot and, it is feared, fatally wounded his wife, Mrs. Ellen Henry, at their residence, near the corner of Elm and Pearl. Although the street was thronged with people nobody could be found able to detail exactly the circumstances of the affair. The most that any of them saw was a young man named Hunter Farrell, whose residence is within two miles of Plano, running out of Henry's yard, closely pursued by Henry, who discharged a pistol at him. At this moment Officer Gains arrested Henry, and Mrs. Henry was seen proceeding from the front door of her residence to King's livery stable, on entering which she dropped on the floor. The stable men carried her back to her residence and sent for Dr. Ayers. An examination of her wound showed that a ball had entered her side, well toward the front and on a line with the heart, leaving little or no hope for her recovery. From several parties in the neighborhood a NEWS reporter learned that three shots had been fired; but an examination of Henry's pistol disclosed only two empty chambers. This fact threw a mystery over the fatal shot, which however, was cleared away by Henry in an interview had with him by a NEWS reporter at the city prison. "I went home," proceeded Mr. Henry, "and found the door locked. I then looked in through a broken pane in a window, but saw nothing. I next kicked the door open, and I found my wife and Hunter Farrell on the bed. I drew my six-shooter in a design to shoot Farrell, but it hung fire, whereupon he ran out of the back door. I then shot my wife, after which I took after Farrell and fired one shot at him. That man once separated myself and my wife, and he and I have carried pistols for one another for nine months. I charge him with visiting my _____ _____ _____ to five times

A Dallas Morning News *article from April 10, 1887 recounts the fatal shooting of Hunter Farrell's mistress, Ellen Henry. Courtesy of the* Dallas Morning News.

decided to leave her husband and move to Dallas. Unfortunately, tragedy struck very early into the journey. While Farrell, Mrs. Henry, and her children were leaving Plano, the team of horses leading the wagon bolted, throwing the Henry's oldest daughter, Lena, out of the wagon and trampling her to death.

The death of Lena kept Mrs. Henry in Plano; however, she felt the residents of Plano had shunned her and again decided to move to Dallas with the children. Mr. Henry joined the family six weeks later, and according to him, they lived "satisfactorily" until neighbors informed him that Farrell had begun visiting the Dallas home. On April 9, 1887, after a year's worth of frustration, suspicion, and heartbreak, Mr. Henry came home to find the two alone together in the bedroom. According to Mr. Henry, he arrived home in the afternoon and found the door to the house locked. After kicking the door open and finding his wife and Farrell on the bed, he attempted to shoot Farrell, but the gun misfired, allowing Farrell time to escape out the door. He then shot his wife and ran after Farrell, firing and missing again.

Mrs. Henry was mortally wounded with the "bullet entering the left side and lodging somewhere in her intestines leaving her in intense agony with little or no hope for her recovery." Four days after the shooting, Ellen Henry died surrounded by her children and neighbors while her husband sat in jail. Mr. Henry was released on bond the day after her death only to be re-arrested after his daughter testified that when she visited him in jail the day before her mother's death he swore that "he wanted to get out, so that he could finish her mother."

In September 1887 while awaiting trial and out on bond, Charles Henry again attacked Farrell with a pistol. For a second time, Farrell's swiftness outshone Henry's shooting abilities, and he once more escaped unscathed. However, speculation surfaced the next day about whether or not Henry was actually the shooter. Despite the preponderance of evidence against him, Henry was later acquitted of the murder of his wife, Ellen. This episode in Farrell's life did not seem to deter him from becoming involved with married women. While Farrell was going through the ordeal of a murdered lover, Mary Alice and Stephen Juhan's marriage began to fall apart.

FREE HAND SHOOTING.

Hunter Farrell on His Way Home Met by Charles Henry, Whose Bad Aim is Lucky for a Third Party.

PLANO, Tex., Sept. 29.—This evening just after dark as Hunter Farrell and Jim Lockhart were walking on their way home, just after crossing the wagon bridge over Spring Creek outside the corporation, they were shot at by a party who had just come out from the brush close to the road, who afterward alleged to be none other than Charles Henry, who is now out on bail for killing his wife in Dallas about four months ago, on account of Hunter Farrell's intimate relations with her. He first fired two shots at Lockhart, just missing his head, when Lockhart hallooed out he was not the right man. Henry then fired two shots at Farrell, who already had a good start and was running for dear life. None of the shots took effect. Parties here state Henry arrived here from Denton on this evening's train. He seemed to be posted as to the time Farrell would pass along the road on his way home. No arrests have been made up to this writing.

The attempted shooting of Hunter Farrell by Charles Henry is discussed in this *Dallas Morning News* article from September 30, 1887. Courtesy of the *Dallas Morning News*.

During a time when divorce was unheard of, Mary Alice and Juhan separated. The divorce papers reveal a sad, troubled relationship. According to divorce documents, Juhan left the family in 1888 to live with another woman, practically abandoning Mary Alice and Ammie. Without any financial support, Mary Alice fell into debt and was forced to open a boardinghouse. She testified in court proceedings that Juhan would periodically return to take her hard-earned cash and squander it. She also claimed Juhan abused her, compelling her to file for divorce.

While running the boardinghouse, Mary Alice met Hunter Farrell. Farrell acted as a witness to the abuse in the divorce proceedings and testified that Mary Alice would provide a better home for Ammie than Juhan. Another witness, Ed Fry, also testified to the same account saying, "the defendant [Juhan] was at almost all times harsh and . . . unkind." Mary Alice's divorce from her first husband is an interesting case when one considers divorce during this period as it demonstrates a woman's difficulty in obtaining a divorce in the nineteenth century. Prior to the beginning of the no-fault divorce in the 1970s, spouses had to sue for divorce on the grounds of adultery, abandonment, cruelty, or on the basis of the other partner committing a crime. In addition to divorces being fairly difficult to obtain, there was a significant amount of shame associated with them.

Juhan never attended the divorce proceedings to dispute the charges of abuse and abandonment. This allowed Mary Alice to be granted the divorce and to maintain custody of Ammie; moreover, Juhan was forced to pay the court costs. Retaining guardianship of Ammie was an unusual factor at the time. During the 1800s, guardianship of the children typically went to the father. However, in the late nineteenth century, the "paternal preference" began to be replaced with a higher regard for maternal nurturing. That Mary Alice retained custody of Ammie is an example of this cultural transition of values surrounding divorce in the United States in the late nineteenth century.

Just one week after her divorce from Juhan, Mary Alice married Hunter T. Farrell on March 5, 1889. In 1890, Hunter bought 124 acres located in Plano, Texas, from Eliza Pittman. One year later, he built the home now known as the Farrell-Wilson house for him, his new bride, and her daughter, Ammie.

The Farrells' affluence was reflected in the opulent Victorian home. Several architectural revival styles were utilized in Texas during the Victorian era. The home is a composite of Victorian era architectural styles such as Second Empire, Carpenter Gothic, and Shingle. The detailing of the house is similar in characteristic to many

Farrell-Wilson House, Plano, Texas

Architectural detail of the Farrell-Wilson
House, Plano, Texas

Side yard of the Farrell-Wilson
House, Plano, Texas

Backyard of the Farrell-Wilson House,
Plano, Texas

of the other homes of wealthy farmers in the area
during the late nineteenth century. A local carpenter,
Robert Abernathy, is believed to have overseen the
construction of the house. Such eclecticism of style
was common in rural areas because of local carpen-
ters' dependence on architectural pattern books and
"a new availability of components from mail-order
catalogues." The advancement of the Industrial
Revolution enabled the progression of Victorian ar-

chitecture into rural areas, where wealthy families, like the Farrells, could purchase elaborate pre-cut trim and incorporate it into their private residences.

The prosperity of Hunter and Mary Alice came from their diversified investments. Although the land surrounding the Plano home was an operational farm until the 1970s, the Farrells did not use it as their main source of income. Farrell invested in gravel businesses and owned several around the Dallas-Fort Worth area. He was also a horse trader, and there was other rental property on the farm.

Farrell was frequently absent from the farmstead because of his business ventures, leaving Mary Alice to make the decisions concerning the farm. Many people who knew Mary Alice described her as having a strong-willed personality and for being a woman who knew what she wanted. She is remembered as always wearing a long black dress and walking through the farm in command.

Ammie Juhan, age sixteen, circa 1896

Despite Farrell's frequent absences from the home and a history of less-than-ethical behavior, he appeared to have a good relationship with his stepdaughter, Ammie, and was said to be "generous" to her. Ammie, in turn, adored him and often referred to him as her father, claiming her maiden name was Farrell, even though he never formally adopted her. Ammie learned one of her favorite pastimes from Farrell, gambling, and continued to be an active poker player her entire life.

Her mannerisms and dress in the late nineteenth century made her appear as the proper Victorian lady, as she was always clothed in the latest fashions. According to Ammie, she attended St. Mary's Girls' School in Dallas, and then finishing school at Ward Belmont in Nashville, Tennessee. The image of Ammie riding on a parade float with other young women stands in sharp contrast to the strong persona she de-

Hunter Farrell gravel train. Courtesy of Candace Morrison Volz.

Drawings done by Ammie Lynch in 1913

Ammie Lynch drives a decorated car for the Midland Commercial Company parade in 1911. The car won first prize.

This first prize loving cup was awarded to Ammie Lynch for the best-decorated car in the Midland Commercial Company parade in 1911.

veloped in her later years. As often happens with young women, Ammie's attention was diverted from familial relations by a young suitor, Woods Lynch.

Ammie married Dr. Woods W. Lynch on November 26, 1901. Less than two years later, the couple had a son, George Hunter, born on October 19, 1903. He was known as "Little Hunter" in honor of Ammie's stepfather. The family moved to Midland, Texas, in 1904, and Dr. Lynch became a well-known physician in the community. He was very involved in the Midland Masonic Lodge and the El Paso Consistory. From outward appearances, the family would have appeared to be the perfect example of matrimonial bliss and success. However, troubles loomed in their home life.

Thirteen years after they were married, Ammie and Dr. Lynch filed for divorce in June 1914. The dispute was bitter and revealed a very unhappy and troublesome marriage. Dr. Lynch claimed Ammie had committed infidelities with one or more men and was unfit to raise young Hunter. Ammie countered that Dr. Lynch was physically abusive to her and Little Hunter, was an alcoholic, tried to coerce her into signing a deed of land over to him, and among various other charges, was addicted to morphine and cocaine. Whichever the case may be, it is ascertainable from the court documents that the divorce between Dr. Lynch and Ammie was brutal.

During the time of the separation, but before the divorce was finalized, Ammie and Little Hunter lived with Mary Alice and Farrell in Plano.

Ammie and Little Hunter,
circa 1904

Above:
Colorado
trip, August
1907. Left
to right:
Mary Alice
Farrell,
Ammie
Lynch, Dr.
Lynch, Little
Hunter, and
unknown.

Woods and Ammie
Lynch, circa 1910

Dr. Lynch wrote as many as three letters a week detailing the pain of his separation from his son. In one dated March 11, 1914, Lynch wrote:

My Dear Man: I had a nice long letter from you just now and was made just as good as could be. But my son I couldn't help but be uneasy when I didn't get a letter for nearly two weeks. Dad thought his man might be sick. You are a real fine boy to be doing so well in school, and I am just as proud of you as a Dad can be of his boy. Dad wants you a great good man and knows now that you will be. I am happy too that you are growing fat and gaining so much in weight. I sure would like to see you and hug you real hard. . . Dad.

The desperation for contact with his son was not only limited to letters to Little Hunter but also with letters to Mary Alice. Letters dated March 5, March 14, and May 20 plead for her to have Hunter write him and for his son to come for a visit. The stress of the divorce and custody battle is apparent in his March 14, 1914, correspondence:

Mrs. Farrell, since going thru what I have and having lost confidence in those whom I had and should have trusted above all, you can see how easily I could lose confidence in others. I am not a normal man anymore; in fact I sometimes think that I am insane. I am not capable of thinking or giving my work the thought and attention it ought to have. I am not capable of mixing with or being sociable with my friends.

I have kept the faith. I have never mentioned my trouble to any person here nor would I permit anyone to mention it to me. Many have asked me about Ammie['s] health and I would always give them an answer as if I knew . . . Ammie wrote Mrs. Hudgins a letter soon after she left. She never mentioned it to me. I don't know what she told her, but she has hardly spoken to me since. But it doesn't matter . . .

Eventually an agreement was made, Ammie was to retain custody of Little Hunter at her mother and stepfather's home in Plano, and Dr. Lynch was to have visitation rights during Little Hunter's breaks from school. However, that agreement quickly changed as Ammie moved forward with her new, single life.

On June 6, 1915, just three months after her divorce was finalized, Ammie and Dudley Moores Wilson became man and wife. Dudley was born in 1885 in Mansfield, Ohio. His father was a "newspaper man," and the family moved frequently in his youth. Around 1900, Dudley moved with his sister Florence to Oklahoma City to live with relatives and finish high school.

W. W. LYNCH, M. D.
MIDLAND, TEX.

March 11, 1914

My Dear Man:—

I had a nice long letter from you just now and was made just as glad as could be. But my son I couldn't help but be mighty when I didn't get a letter for nearly two weeks. Dad thought his man might be sick.

You are a real fine boy to be doing so well in school and I am just as proud of you as a Dad can be of his boy. Dad wants you a great good man and knows now that you will be. I am happy too that you are growing fat and gaining so much in weight. I sure would like to see you and hug you real hard.

I am glad that Queen is allright and that you are taking good care of her, I haven't seen Mary Lou since you left. I will send your gun and tackle with the Spotted tiger real soon. Remember man that its against the law to shoot a high power like the 25–35 in Collin County and several other counties of the state.

John Wagman came in to see me yesterday and asked for your address saying he was going to write to you. We had another sand storm yesterday and another last night.

Dad is going to run down to see you some Saturday and spend the day with his boy. You and Jim can run down to Dallas and we will all take in the moving pictures.

I am awfully sorry Papa Hunter has been so sick, and hope he will soon be sound and well.

I will bring the money for your school when I come on and may wait till then to bring the guns and fishing tackle.

Be a good sweet boy and write Dad when you can.

With lots of love, hugs & kisses

Dad.

Letter from Dr. Lynch to his son, Little Hunter, March 11, 1914

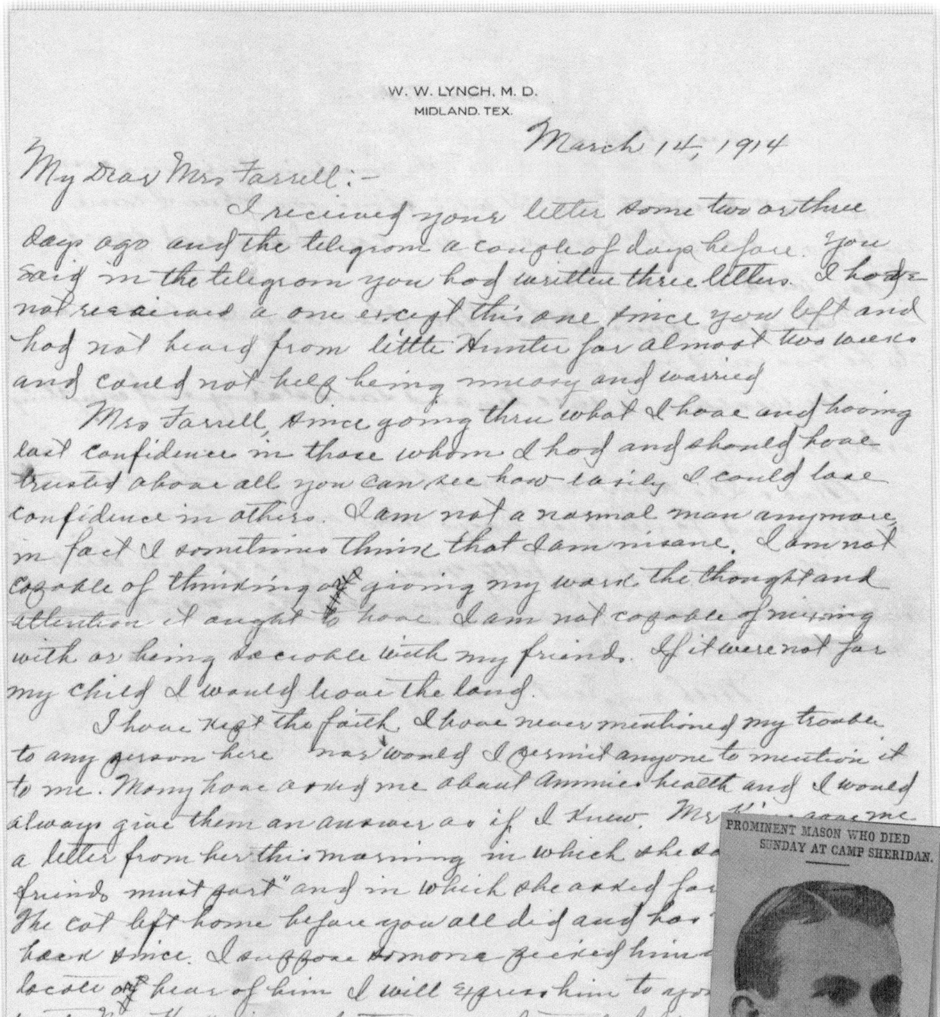

W. W. LYNCH, M. D.
MIDLAND, TEX.

March 14, 1914

My Dear Mrs Farrell:-

I recieved your letter some two or three days ago and the telegram a couple of days before. You said in the telegram you had written three letters. I have not received a one except this one since you left and had not heard from little Hunter for almost two weeks and could not help being uneasy and worried.

Mrs Farrell, since going thru what I have and having lost confidence in those whom I had and should have trusted above all you can see how easily I could lose confidence in others. I am not a normal man anymore in fact I sometimes think that I am insane. I am not capable of thinking or giving my work the thought and attention it ought to have. I am not capable of mixing with or being sociable with my friends. If it were not for my child I would leave the land.

I have kept the faith. I have never mentioned my trouble to any person here nor would I permit anyone to mention it to me. Many have asked me about Annie's health and I would always give them an answer as if I knew. Mrs ... me a letter from her this morning in which she sa... friends must part" and in which she asked fo... The cat left home before you all did and has ... back since. I suppose someone picked him ... locate or hear of him I will express him to yo... wrote Mrs Hudgins a letter soon after she left. ... it to me. I don't know what she told her, but ... spoken to me since. But it doesn't matter.

Well there is no news worth mentioning, ... the place at 3500.00 tho there is no market ... of property and have no idea it can be sold. ... me yesterday to know if I would rent it as a ...

PROMINENT MASON WHO DIED SUNDAY AT CAMP SHERIDAN.

MAJOR W. W. LYNCH.

Major Woodsy W. Lynch died at Camp Sheridan, Montgomery, Ala., Sunday, June 9. He was for several years a prominent physician of Midland, Texas, and was active in Masonic work, being a member of Midland Lodge and El Paso Consistory. When war was declared against Germany he enlisted and was commissioned a Captain and stationed with the medical corps at El Paso. He was subsequently promoted to the rank of Major and transferred to Camp Sheridan, where he remained in active charge of hospital and army work until a few days prior to his death.

The body will arrive in Dallas from New Orleans today. Major Lynch was a brother of Mrs. A. C. Parker, 3426 Beverly drive. The funeral services will be conducted at the residence of A. C. Parker tomorrow at 10 o'clock. The Rev. John G. Slater of the East Dallas Christian Church will officiate. The services will be in charge of Dallas Masons.

Above: Letter from Dr. Lynch to Mary Alice Farrell, March 14, 1914.
Right: Dr. Woods Lynch obituary, 1918. Courtesy of the *Dallas Morning News*.

He graduated from Colorado School of Mines with a degree in mining, engineering, and metallurgy. He worked for Texas Power and Light Company and later opened his own civil engineering company. He also spent time as an engineer for the Texas Highway Department.

Dudley Wilson, circa 1920s   Ammie Wilson, circa 1920s

After his marriage to Ammie in 1915, the couple moved to the Munger District of Dallas. With Dudley traveling a great deal for his job, it gave Ammie the freedom to pursue her personal interests. This included spending a great deal of time in the town of Mineral Wells at the Baker Hotel. She quickly settled into this new, unrestricted married life.

The United States' involvement in World War I would soon take a toll on Little Hunter and his relationship with his father. Shortly after the United States declared war on Germany, Dr. Lynch enlisted in the army and was stationed with the medical corps at El Paso, Texas, as a captain. He was then promoted to major and reassigned to Camp Sheridan in Alabama. While stationed in Alabama, Dr. Lynch became ill and died June 9, 1918. He left behind a new wife, Lois Stillwell Lynch, and his son, Hunter Lynch. An American Legion Post was named in his honor in Midland, Texas.

Although the relationship between Ammie and Dr. Lynch had withered, it is unclear how the relationship between father and son remained, as there are no surviving letters after 1914. However, Dr. Lynch's death undoubtedly had a profound effect on his son as it left him without parental influence for the most part. Ammie had moved away from Plano when she married Dudley and left Little Hunter to be reared by his grandmother. When Dr. Lynch died, his estate and government pension went to his son. For unspecified reasons, Ammie turned over legal guardianship of Little Hunter to Mary Alice, due to his still being a minor at the time of his father's death. Mary Alice became his temporary guardian until he became of legal age.

NOTICE BY PUBLICATION OF FINAL ACCOUNT.

The State of Texas.

To the Sheriff or any Constable of Collin County—GREETING:

Mrs. Alice Farrell, Guardian, of the Estate of George Hunter Lynch, minor, having filed in our County Court his FINAL ACCOUNT of the condition of the Estate of said George Hunter Lynch, Minor, together with an application to be discharged from said Guardianship.

You Are Hereby Commanded, That by publication of this Writ for twenty days in a newspaper regularly published in the County of Collin you give due notice to all persons interested in the Account of Final Settlement of said Estate, to file their objections thereto, if any they have, on or before the June Term, 1924 of said County Court, commencing and to be holden at the Court House of said County, in the City of McKinney, Texas on the First Monday in June A. D. 1924, when said Account and Application will be considered by said Court.

Witness MINNIE BURRAGE, Clerk of the County Court of Collin County.

Given under my hand and seal of said Court, at my office in the City of McKinney, Texas, this 14th day of April A. D. 1924.

MINNIE BURRAGE, Clerk C. C. Collin Co. (Seal) By J. OLLIE SMITH, Deputy Clerk.

This newspaper notice reports that Little Hunter is no longer a minor and under the guardianship of his grandmother, Mary Alice. Courtesy of *Plano Star Courier.*

Hunter Lynch on a donkey

Hunter Lynch, age six, sent this postcard to his grandmother, Mary Alice Farrell, in 1909.

Hunter Lynch, circa 1910

During this time, the nearly forty-year marriage of Mary Alice and Farrell was falling apart. Farrell was absent for long periods of time dealing with his gravel business, and Mary Alice argued that this put a strain on their marriage. Leading up to and after their divorce, Farrell was involved in eight court cases relating to land disputes, monies owed, and his gravel businesses. However, that was not the only reason Farrell was in and out of the courtroom. He had two lawsuits against him claiming infidelity with several married women. These indiscretions seem more likely for the filing of divorce then his absence from the Plano home. Whatever the exact reasoning, the couple divorced in 1928. This was the second divorce for the "independent" Mary Alice, in a time when divorce was still considered "taboo."

Texas's history as a community property state regulated that Mary Alice was entitled to keep half of the earnings acquired of their joint interests during their marriage, meaning Mary Alice received half of the community property, including their Plano home. The fight between Farrell and Mary Alice for the property became exceedingly hostile, with allegations of misconduct and the filing of four separate lawsuits by Mary Alice. In two lawsuits, she claimed Farrell was withholding land and monetary assets, equaling $325,000, while in a separate lawsuit she alleged he had sown the land at the Plano farm with Johnson grass in the middle of the night in 1930 intent on damaging the fields. Although Farrell was found not guilty on the Johnson grass charge, acquaintances often believed she had won.

Despite the fact Little Hunter had been raised in a home of hostile divorces, it did not embitter his romantic notions. In April 1927, Hunter married Mamie Myrtle "Johnny" O'Neal. However, their blissful six-year marriage was cut short by Hunter's death in 1933 from esophageal septicemia and stomatitis thought to be caused by alcohol addiction. His death at the young age of twenty-nine had a profound and lasting impact upon his family. Johnny got along well with Ammie and Mary Alice and continued to live on the farm for a year after Hunter's death. She moved back to her parents' home in 1934 but continued to keep in contact with the family through the 1970s.

In 1934, shortly after her last court case, Mary Alice passed away from a cerebral hemorrhage. In her will, she left Ammie life tenancy, meaning she could live on the Plano farm for the remainder of her life but would never own it. Mary Alice Farrell was a unique woman in the time that she lived. When women were struggling to be viewed as individuals, she twice divorced and fought to maintain her independence. In the end, her giving nature was revealed through the donation of her property to charitable causes. The property was to be divided in equal shares between the Buckner's Orphan Home of Dallas and the National Benevolent Association of the Christian Church in St. Louis, Missouri, in memory of her grandson, Hunter Lynch. She requested that her epitaph simply read, "I have always tried to be just to my fellow man."

Hunter with his new bride, Johnny O'Neal Lynch, circa 1927

After the divorce from Mary Alice was finalized, Farrell married his secretary, Doris Maude Morrison, on May 30, 1930. Doris was a once-divorced woman, forty years his junior and from a wealthy Dallas real estate development family. The couple seemed to have a compatible marriage as Doris was a shrewd businesswoman and helped run many of her husband's gravel businesses and properties. The couple bought a home in the affluent Highland Park District of Dallas, and Doris's mother, Maude White Morrison, lived in the home until her death in 1941. The Farrells had a very short marriage as Hunter died of renal disease in 1936. Doris passed away in 1953 of uterine cancer.

Mary Alice Farrell, circa 1930

Hunter Farrell at one of his gravel pits. Courtesy of Candace Morrison Volz.

Home of Hunter and Doris Farrell, 3710 Potomac Avenue, Dallas, Texas. Courtesy of Candace Morrison Volz.

This pastel drawing of Hunter Lynch was from a photograph taken during his 1928 hunting trip to Mexico; the artist is unknown.

Hunter Lynch

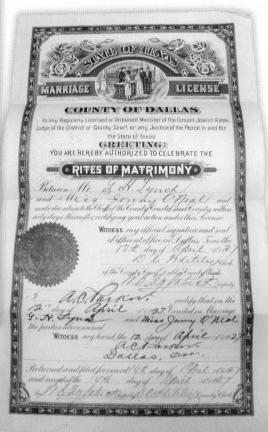

George Hunter Lynch and Johnny O'Neal's marriage license

Hunter Lynch poses during a hunting trip to Mexico, 1928.

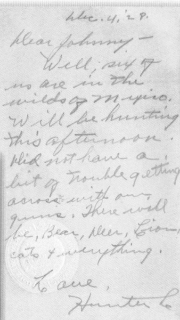

While on a hunting trip to Mexico in 1928, Hunter sent this postcard to Johnny.

This pastel drawing of Hunter Lynch was from a photograph taken during his 1928 hunting trip to Mexico; the artist is unknown.

Hunter Lynch sits on a car.

Hunter Lynch

Lynch wedding party, June 1927. Left to right: Anna Lee, Jason Hayes, Flora Mae, unknown, Johnny Lynch, and Hunter Lynch.

Hunter Lynch died at the age of twenty-nine on January 31, 1933.

HUNTER LYNCH OF PLANO CLAIMED BY GRIM REAPER

DIED IN DALLAS HOSPITAL TUESDAY MORNING—WAS 29 YEARS OLD

George Hunter Lynch, aged 29 years, 3 months and 12 days, died in St. Paul Hospital, Dallas, Tuesday morning at 5:50 o'clock. He had been a patient in Hot Springs, Arkansas, for a few weeks, and was brought to the Dallas hospital a few days ago.

The deceased was born in Plano October 19th, 1903.

He is survived by his widow, Mrs. Johnny Lynch, his mother, Mrs. Annie E. Wilson and his grandmother, Mrs. Mary Alice Farrell, all of Plano.

Funeral services were held at the home of Mrs. Farrell, two miles west of Plano, Wednesday afternoon at 2 o'clock, conducted by Rev. D. W. Nicholas, pastor of the Plano Christian church.

Interment followed in Restland Memorial Park.

* * *

Pallbearers were:

Active—Lex Newbill, Francis Thompson, Roy Carpenter, Russell Carpenter, Fred Harrington, Jr., and W. L. Crawford, III.

Honorary—Fred Harrington, Sr., D. S. Caleman, Dr. John O. McReynolds, Dr. Tom M. Kirgsey, Dr. R. L. Rutherford, W. M. Chaddick, J. H. Gulledge, Ed Allen, Will Hedgcoxe, W. O. Haggard, J. L. Toone, Ben Garrett, Johnnie Shipp and Tommie Lovell.

Plano Star Courier obituary for George Hunter Lynch, February 2, 1933. Courtesy of the *Plano Star Courier.*

GEORGE H. LYNCH, NATIVE OF PLANO, DIES HERE TUESDAY

Funeral rites will be held Wednesday afternoon at Plano, Texas, for George Hunter Lynch, 29, native of Plano, who died Tuesday morning at a Dallas hospital.

The services will be at 2 o'clock at the home of Mrs. Mary Alice Farrell, with Dr. D. W. Nicholas officiating. Interment will be in Restland Memorial park.

Surviving are his widow, Mrs. Johnny Lynch; his mother and his grandmother, Mrs. Farrell, all of Plano.

Active pallbearers will be Lex Newbill, Francis Thompson, Roy Carpenter, Russell Carpenter, Fred Harrington, Jr., and W. L. Crawford, III. Honorary pallbearers will be Fred Harrington, Sr., D. S. Coleman, Dr. John O. McReynolds, Dr. Tom M. Kirksey, Dr. R. L. Rutherford, C. M. Chaddick, J. H. Gulledge, Ed Allen, Will Hodgecoxe, W. O. Haggard, J. L. Toone, Ben Garrett, Johnnie Shipp and Tommie Lovell.

If a man is always on the go he seldom stops when he gets there.

Dallas Times Herald obituary for George Hunter Lynch. Courtesy of the *Dallas Times Herald.*

IN REPLY
REFER TO

PHONE 2-4076

HEADQUARTERS 411TH FIELD ARTILLERY
OFFICE OF THE UNIT INSTRUCTOR
530-32 FEDERAL BUILDING

DALLAS, TEXAS

Feb. 2, 1933.

Dear Johnny & Granny:

Pardon this letter to you at a time like this, but there were a few things I wanted to say to you yesterday, but just couldn't do it.

The news of Hunter's death came as a shock to me, for I did not know that he was seriously sick. I had heard that he had gone to Hot Springs and thought he was still there. The first news I had was when I read the announcement in the Herald. Am indeed sorry that I did not get to see him, as I counted him as my very best friend.

I believe you both know that there wasn't a thing on earth that I wouldn't have done for Hunter, and I want you both, as well as Mrs. Wilson, to feel free to call on me if there is anything whatsoever that I can do for you. It just occurred to me that there might be something or other here in town, or elsewhere, that I could do for you.

With sincerest sympathy in this, your hour of great sorrow,

As always,

Ned

Upon Hunter's death, his friend, Ned, expresses his condolences in this letter to Johnny Lynch and Mary Alice Farrell. Inset: Hunter Lynch's grave at Restland Cemetery, Dallas, Texas.

Juanita Sanders

The history of the Farrell family has been discussed at length; however, there were many other families who lived on the farm and also considered it their home. A majority of the families living on the property were tenement farmers and lived in small, one- or two-room dwellings scattered around the 365 acres. Most of the families were African American and did not remain on the farm for extended periods of time. This pattern of short-term involvement was primarily due to limited job opportunities, the mobility of African American families during the early twentieth century, substandard educational prospects, racial violence, Jim Crow laws, and disenfranchisement.

The Sanders family broke this pattern of short-term residency as Ernest worked for the family for twenty-seven years. Ernest was the son of a former slave, Edward Sanders, who moved to Collin County in 1891 with his former slave-owner from Tennessee. Ernest attended school at Shiloh Baptist Church, and his family worked on the Farrell farm. Upon returning from World War I, he was hired in 1920 as the farm manager and began living on the property in a small, one-bedroom house with a kitchen, which was built in 1915. As the absence of Hunter Farrell became more and more pronounced, Ernest began to take on a greater responsibility of running and managing the farm, from helping with the threshing to handling the financial responsibilities of paying the daily wages to the cotton pickers. The fondness between Ernest and Mary Alice was evident. When she died, Mary Alice left him a 1934 Chevrolet Coupe automobile in her will.

After Mary Alice's death, her daughter, Ammie Wilson, became the matriarch of the household, and she depended on Ernest's knowledge over her own farming inexperience. Ernest married Juanita Watkins in June 1936, and she soon joined her husband on the farm. Juanita helped Ammie with cleaning the house and other household chores. She churned the butter until the family

Ernest Sanders with his daughter, Ammie

began buying it, and she often felt as if she had the house to herself since Ammie was frequently absent from the home for sheep shows. Nevertheless, Juanita acknowledged that Ammie cherished her position as "lord of that domain." Indeed, the house did flourish during the years Ammie lived there; she rejuvenated the house, filling it with roses, "booze decanters," pictures of her sheep, and her award ribbons. The ongoing close relationship between the Sanders and Farrell-Wilson families is evident as Ernest and Juanita named their daughter Ammie Ellen.

Juanita Sanders with her daughter, Ammie

Ammie Sanders

Three of the Sanders children, left to right: Jimmy, Steve, and Glenn

Ammie Wilson on the back porch of her house with her namesake, Ammie Sanders

2

Ammie's Sheep Business

Ammie Wilson with a baby lamb

The pain from the death of her only son had a devastating impact on Ammie in 1933. To cope with her loss, she found a hobby to occupy her time. She began to raise sheep as a tribute to one of the last gifts her son had given her a year before his death, a baby lamb, and "from the desperate longing of her crushed heart, she could find solace only in the thing her child loved most—that little pet sheep." Traditionally, the family had raised cattle, so Ammie had to learn about the sheep industry from scratch. In 1941, she started on the show circuit with six Hampshire sheep, on the suggestion of an acquaintance who often gave her technical advice in the early years. Dudley did not understand his wife's affinity for raising sheep as she once stated, "he thinks the woman should rock the cradle, instead of raise sheep, but he furnishes the bankroll for the project and that's the most important thing."

From 1941 on, Ammie's life was dedicated to her thriving sheep business. She believed that "if you are going to raise show sheep, you might as well raise good ones." Her flock grew to be one of the largest in the United States, and she was the only woman breeder in Texas. She was said to be so thorough with her flock that she attended each one's birth and claimed to treat each one "just like a baby." One hundred breeding ewes were kept, and each one had a name and number, which she knew. She even named all of her sheep after famous people. "I have an Ike Eisenhower named because he is a natural-born boss. His twin is Chester Nimitz." When someone beat her at a show, she would immediately write a check to buy the animal so that she could "bring the winner home with her." In the 1940s, Ammie was the head of the Collin County Purebred Livestock Association. Her dedication to the sheep and her competitive spirit were intertwined. She said that she would rather place low in international competitions than win first at other shows.

Ammie with her award-winning Hampshire sheep

Bill Raiden had been working on the farm as a shepherd for Ammie until the retirement of Ernest Sanders in 1947 when he was promoted to herdsman. One friend wrote that Ammie practically raised Bill and considered herself a motherly figure for him. When Ammie discovered he had a girlfriend, Jacquelynn Harper, she was, at first, not too happy about it; eventually she warmed to the idea and remodeled the caretaker's house for them to live in once they were married.

Collin County Purebred Livestock Association 1941, courtesy of the Frances Bates Wells Collection, Plano Public Library

Ammie quickly came to depend on the Raiden family and relied on Bill to help with most aspects of her sheep business. Ammie once rode in a truck with Bill from Plano to Chicago for the 1952 show at the Chicago State Fair. Countless friends, acquaintances, and newspaper reports mentioned that wherever Ammie went with her sheep, Bill was right beside her.

This is not to imply her husband, Dudley, did not accompany his wife on the circuit; to the contrary, however, Dudley had a "casual interest" in his wife's sheep business. He was an unassuming character who always indulged in his wife's wishes.

Ammie poses with her prize-winning sheep at the Southwestern Exposition and Fat Stock Show in Fort Worth, Texas, 1958. Courtesy of Ammie Wilson Papers, Texas Tech University, Lubbock, Texas.

Ammie feeds a sheep on the farm.

Ammie Wilson

He slept in a separate small room above the kitchen that adjoined Ammie's suite. He once tried his hand at raising chickens to sell, but the business floundered. Ammie once noted, "he's not much interested in sheep . . . but [he] serves as the power behind the throne when the bankroll runs short."

During her life in Plano, Ammie was described as an affable woman. With her easy humor, she developed friends at her sheep shows every year. Within the sheep industry she was described as "refreshing." She was the kind of person who stayed the whole evening with her friend Mae Ross when Mae's son was killed during World War II. An acquaintance of Ammie's, E.A. Randles, described her as a "friendly and helpful person, but one who could get tough when it was required." Her shrewdness was also well documented. It was said that she was a tough businesswoman who practiced Christian principles and was honest. Known for her assertiveness and ego, she "demanded perfection," and only Dudley seemed capable of indulging her domineering nature.

Her competitiveness was well rewarded. In 1946, she "pulled down her first grand champion," and in that same year, she set a record by selling one of her Hampshire sheep for $1,200. During 1951 and 1952, Ammie swept almost every major show, including the Texas State Fair. In 1952, she won first prize at the International Livestock Exhibition in Chicago, resulting in her biggest win to date. Of that win, she said, "the International is the big one, and that's what I had my heart set on." She won six consecutive times at the Houston Fat Stock Show.

Ammie was not modest about her wins: during that period, she estimated that she had thousands of blue ribbons in her trophy room. By 1955, she had 300 in her flock of sheep and had won two International prizes. In 1954, upon winning the Dallas Altrusa Club Mature Woman Award, Ammie said, "I chose a man's work so that I could prove that I can do as good or better job than they do . . . I will get out of this business when I am too old to dream." She was described as "a liberated woman before the . . . leaders of the movement were even born."

Ammie appeared on the cover of *Sheep and Goat Raiser* magazine in January 1952.

Ammie received much attention for her involvement in the sheep industry as a woman and as an excellent sheep breeder. The sheer amount of press coverage is evidence of this, and she thrived in the attention. She was a regular on Don McNeill's *Breakfast Club* show from Chicago and got great delight out of appearing on the hit television show *What's My Line* in 1951. Much to their dismay, the panel was unable to guess what Ammie's profession was.

In addition to her friendly but assertive nature, Ammie was flamboyant and liked to spend her wealth. She spent large amounts of money on the sheep, drove nice cars, and at one point owned a pink Lincoln Coupe. She spent a lot of her time traveling in "exclusive European circles." In the mid-1950s, she took a break from showing sheep to take a trip around the world. She once told a reporter that despite her money she continued to work because she could not remain idle and said, "Where's the fun in that?"

Indeed, Ammie Wilson had a variety of activities to keep her from getting bored. Among her favorite activities was playing poker. Although her famous poker games were

Hampshire sheep

Ammie with her prize-winning sheep

Ammie E. Wilson Award for the American Hampshire Sheep Association at the American Royal Livestock Show for Champion Hampshire Ram, 1969–1985.

American Royal Premier Hampshire Breeder Award, 1963

Ammie Wilson took command, in both wins and attitude, at every show she attended.

Ammie in her trophy room showcasing her awards. Courtesy of *Sheep and Goat Raiser*, January 1952.

American Royal Premier Hampshire Breeder Award, 1965.

Part II   The Dallas Morning News   Saturday, March 13, 1954

NEW BLUE RIBBON

Prize-Winning Farm Woman Gets Altrusa Club Award

By MARY BRINKERHOFF

The Wilson Farm near Plano, famed for blue-ribbon sheep, had a grand champion of a different kind Friday.

Mrs. Ammie E. Wilson, 72-year-old farm owner and former Dallas resident, was named winner of the Dallas Altrusa Club's Mature Woman Award. She will receive an inscribed plaque at a dinner Tuesday in the French Room of Hotel Adolphus.

Each year the club honors a woman who has founded a new business or changed her occupation after the age of forty and has made a success of the work for five years. Judges also consider whether a candidate has demonstrated a positive interest in others. Mrs. Wilson more than qualifies on all counts.

At the age of sixty, having farmed her parents' 500 acres for eight years, she launched her sheep-raising venture with six fine Hampshires. Today she owns 200 sheep and cares for them almost singlehanded now that her shepherd has been called into service. Her well-tended animals have brought her a sheaf of prizes and nationwide publicity.

A past president of the Collin County Purebred Livestock Association, Mrs. Wilson has long been active in 4-H Club work. She and her fellow ranchers furnish boys with calves, hogs and sheep to use in starting their livestock careers. The veteran prizewinner, sometimes called the Southwest's premier sheepwoman, never places her animals in competition with those of a boy whom she has helped.

Interviewed by telephone at her home Friday, Mrs. Wilson said that her name was submitted to the Altrusa Club by the Plano Business and Professional Women's Club while she was on a livestock-show circuit. She knew nothing of the nomination until her return.

"Now, children, don't be too disappointed when I lose," she admonished those who told her.'

This philosophical attitude extends to Mrs. Wilson's theories on opportunities for women in a man's world.

"Any business you undertake is going to be a problem, because the men have forgotten more than you know. But with application and hard work you can do anything you want—anything at all.

"I pity women who don't undertake something worthwhile; if I had a million dollars I'd still be working. I'd hate to pass out of the world without having a single good deed. That's where you get your pleasure."

The farm boss' husband, Dudley Wilson, won't be able to attend the dinner Tuesday. He must take time off from his duties as a civil and mining engineer to help out at the farm. "It's lambing time, you know."

It was while he was on assignments in Central and South America that Mrs. Wilson lived in Dallas. In 1933 their only son died, and the couple determined to continue operation of the farm which was to have been his. As she puts it, "I decided I wouldn't run for cover."

Now the farm produces wheat, oats, corn, maize and cattle, but to Mrs. Wilson it's the sheep that matter. She feels that a herd's calling has a spiritual dimension. "The work keeps me a little closer to God."

—Associated Press Wirephoto.

Dallas Altrusa Club's Mature Woman Award for will go to 72-year-old Mrs. Ammie E. Wilson, raises prize sheep near Plano. She is pictured e with one of her champions, Joan Crawford by

This *Dallas Morning News* article features Ammie and her achievement in winning the Altrusa Mature Woman Award, March 13, 1954. Courtesy of the *Dallas Morning News*.

Ammie feeds a baby lamb at her Plano, Texas, farm.

"scandalous" to some of the women in the Plano community, men and women from Dallas attended and joined in the games. During the rounds, she pulled down the shades and lit a cigar. It was said that the only time Ammie played unfairly was during these games. She got amusement out of inviting all the gamblers in the community and giving them as much liquor as they could consume before the games to gain an advantage. Additionally, she drove into Dallas every Thursday to play poker with her girlfriends.

In many ways, Ammie was not interested in being confined into the traditional roles of women. She liked to drink whiskey and smoke cigars at her poker parties, and raising sheep was definitely a male-dominated field. She gained acceptance at the sheep shows by playing games of craps with the men. Her language was crude and described as "salty." E.A. Randles depicted Ammie's personality as:

The expression "I wish I were a man" is used to cover many situations, from frustrations to inadequaties [sic]. A youth tormented by the local bully conjures in his mind the day he is a man and defends himself to victory. A mother under duress declares, "if I were a man, I would give you the threshing of your life," to an [sic] wayward son. Many young ladies aspiring to unattainable heights in atheletics [sic] cry in despair, "I wish I were a man." And then there is the woman who wants to excell [sic] in the once regarded "man's world," thinks it unfair that because of the lack of acceptance, physical strength, psychological barriers, etc., and if I were a man all these barriers would be erased. Miss Ammie should have been a man. Married to a brilliant and compassonite [sic] engineer, her mailbox read "Ammie E. Wilson" only.

—The Times Herald Staff Photo

LITTLE BO-PEEP at 73 is Mrs. Ammie E. Wilson of Plano, who holds an orphan lamb at her farm. Mrs. Wilson Friday was named Mature Woman of the Year by the Dallas Altrusa Club.

73-Year-Old Woman

Plano Sheepraiser Wins Annual Altrusa Award

By Jane Hardison
The Times Herald Staff Writer

A 73-year-old Plano woman who chose a man's job after she was 60 will quit when she is "too old to dream."

Mrs. Ammie E. Wilson of Plano Friday morning was named the Mature Woman of the year by the Dallas Altrusa Club for her success in the business world after the age of 40.

She will receive a citation at the Altrusa award dinner at 7 p. m. Tuesday at the Adolphus Hotel.

"I chose a man's work so that I could prove that I can do as good or better job than they do," she said Friday at her farm.

"I will get out of this business when I am too old to dream." she said.

It is the middle of lambing season and Mrs. Wilson has extra chores this year. She and her husband, Dudley, are caring for the stock alone. Just after the February showings, their herdsman was drafted.

To add to the chores there are several orphan lambs to feed. And her husband's major business interests are elsewhere.

"It took me five years, from

See SHEEP RAISER on Page 4.

The *Dallas Times Herald* wrote about Ammie winning the Altrusa Mature Woman Award in March 1954. Courtesy of the *DallasTimes Herald*.

Ammie and Dudley Wilson in their home, Plano, Texas

From left to right, Johnny Lynch, Dudley Wilson, Ammie Wilson, Johnny's sister (Lola), and Florence Wilson enjoy a dinner party at the Wilson home.

Her appearance was reflective of her eccentric personality. There are very few accounts of Ammie that fail to mention her attire and stature. She was a small woman with reddish hair that later turned to blondish gray. She had a strong, "smiling face" and gold teeth. She also had one glass eye, which she wore sunglasses to cover. In 1925 Ammie was blinded by cataracts; she underwent a series of operations but eventually lost one eye. It was obvious to all, but she never mentioned it.

Ammie's wardrobe instantly defined her personality to people. They "were in character for a rancher." She claimed to own only one dress, which she wore to church. Her custom-made high-heeled boots were ordered from Fort Worth, and it was reported that several pairs of her boots were always lined up in the hallway of the house. Her clothes were colorful and expensive. She wore western-style pants, shirts with pearl snaps, and a large Stetson hat or a long-billed cap "generally signifying she meant business—there's show work coming up." Although she liked trousers, boots, and Stetson hats, she also liked diamonds and furs. One acquaintance declared she carried loose diamonds in her pocket, a claim no one can confirm. When she appeared on *What's My Line*, she wore a Dior suit, a mink coat, "eight-carat diamond ring and a diamond-studded wedding band on her left hand, and an exquisite pearl dinner ring on the other, a diamond collar button, a jeweled brooch, and pearl and diamond earrings."

Though Ammie loved to dress herself extravagantly, as a married couple, she and Dudley were very charitable. She made her sheep available to the Future Farmers of America (FFA), paid for their annual banquet, and served as an FFA sponsor. She often helped to finance education for young men who worked hard. When a woman whose husband had deserted her and their children came by the house, Ammie offered to let them stay in one of her tenant houses and "kept them two years." She brought the girls from the Juliet Fowler Christian Children's Home to her house and treated them to new clothes. She contributed $5,000 to the building fund of the First Christian Church of Plano.

Toward the end of his life, Dudley remained close to the farmstead for the majority of the time. However, in 1968, Dudley and Ammie were traveling to the Iowa State Fair when they were involved in a horrific car accident on August 18. Ammie sustained a broken hip and was flown to Dallas for her injuries. She eventually recovered, but was never quite the same. Unfortunately, Dudley died several days after the accident on August 25, 1968. The couple had been married fifty-three years.

In 1961, Ammie wrote, "Whatever you do, don't say I'm a good girl. Folks will laugh. This may be my last year, but I'll take all bets." This statement reveals the vivacious personality of Ammie Wilson, and even as she aged, her sense of humor remained intact. While in a hospital, she told a priest that he need not worry about praying for her because "the preachers over there at the Christian Church have been praying for me for 50 years. If they haven't got the job done by now, I doubt there's anything more you can do." She would in fact live another eleven years until 1972 when she died of congestive heart failure. An acquaintance, Paul Carter, said at the time of her death: "She was a unique person—one of a kind. A Texan in the classic mold. Her passing is like an era in history that is gone, and we are saddened by it." Eddie Stimpson Jr.,

Dudley Wilson

Services Held

Funeral services for Dudley Moores Wilson will be held today at 2 p. m. in the First Christian Church of Plano.

Rev. Morris Beard, church pastor, will officiate, Internment will be made in Restland Memorial Park under the direction of the Harrington Funeral Home.

Mr. Wilson died Sunday morning, August 25, in Mercy Hospital, Des Moines, Iowa, as the result of injuries received August 18 in an automobile accident near Des Moines.

He and Mrs. Wilson were en route to the Iowa State Fair when the accident occurred. Mrs. Wilson, who received extensive injuries, was flown to Dallas Monday afternoon and has been a patient in Medical Arts Hospital in Dallas.

Born July 25, 1885 in Mansfield, Ohio, Mr. Wilson was 83 years, 1 month old at the time of his death.

He was an honor graduate of the Colorado School of Mines with a degree in mining engineering and metelurgy. He was formerly with the Texas Power & Light Company and later organized his own civil engineering construction company.

On June 6, 1915 he was married to Ammie E. Wilson and the couple had since resided on their farm just west of Plano on Farm to Market Road 544 where they raised prize winning sheep.

Mr. Wilson was a member of the National Mining and Engineering Society, a member of the Plano Chamber of Commerce and the First Christian Church of Plano.

Survivors are his wife; Mrs. Ammie Wilson of Plano, and a sister, Miss Florence Wilson of Oklahoma City, Oklahoma.

Dallas Morning News obituary for Dudley Wilson. Courtesy of the Dallas Morning News.

Ammie and Dudley Wilson

Plano, Texas,
August 11, 1968.

Dear Johnny,

I am ashamed that so far I have failed to acknowledge receipt of the
birth day cards and gifts from you and Miss Lila.

We have been snowed under making hay and getting it hauled. It rained
so often, but we saved it all and have all the barns and building up town
full.

We have both been pretty well and I am delighted that Ammie has done so well
It is a job to keep up with her and not let her over do. Have gotten together
a small show flock and really they are good. They are parked at Roy Warrick's
place in Oscaloosa, Iowa. It is so much cooler up there. Roy is crazy about
Ammie and getting her a good show flock. He has them entered at the Iowa State
Fair in Des Moines. I am driving her up to Des Moines this coming Saturday
to see them show. Then come home quick as we can. Alex McKenzie will help Roy's
boy show them and Billy stay here this trip. Roy had a heart attack and we
nearly lost him this f spring. Alex and Roy's boyhelped on the whole deal.

Ammie needs something to keep her interested and not just work so hard in
house and kitchen.

I am feeling good, only got some new glasses couple days ago, but they not
fitted good. Everyone so busy do not get a job done right. Old doctor Newton
sold out to a new young fellow and wonder if he is OK. One thing he does not
recommend having and cateract operation .

Maybe we will get some of the work done up and can get together with you folks.

You should not have been so generous with my birthday but I do appreciate it
a lot.

Hope you all are well and can keep cool enough.

Lots of love of love.

Dudley

Dudley Wilson sent this letter to Johnny Lynch, August 11, 1968, one week before his fatal car accident.

COMFORT

Oh, deem not they are blest alone
Whose lives a peaceful tenor keep;
The Power who pities man has shown
A blessing for the eyes that weep.

The light of smiles shall fill again
The lids that overflow with tears;
And weary hours of woe and pain
Are promises of happier years.

For God has marked each sorrowing day,
And numbered every secret tear,
And heaven's long age of bliss shall pay
For all his children suffer here.

WILLIAM CULLEN BRYANT

In Memory of
MRS. AMMIE WILSON

Born: June 24, 1884
Cresson, Texas

Died: November 23, 1972
Dallas, Texas

Services:
Saturday, November 25, 1972, 2 P. M.
First Christian Church
Plano, Texas

Officiating:
Rev. Morris Beard

Music:
Soloist: Mr. Keith Cannon
Organist: Mrs. Larry Taylor

Pallbearers:
Rob Harrington   Johnny Hull
Don Clark   Bud Millraney
John Wells   Ben Garrett

Interment:
Restland Memorial Park
Dallas, Texas

Under the direction of
Harrington - Bratcher
Funeral Home

Plano, Texas

Ammie E. Wilson memorial card

a longtime friend who had worked on the farm for many years, described Ammie in his 1996 book, *My Remembers*, as:

Miss Ammie Wilson was a strong hard-core woman who had something else going for her. She was a beautiful woman. But she did not let the beauty go to her head. You would have to look into her eyes and see the smile on her lips only to feel that behind those eyes and underneath that smile, down underneath that beauty, she had kindness, she had love, and she had care and concern about the peoples she came in contact with. . . I have no regrets about meeting this woman who kept her beauty hid under a straw hat tied down with a scarf, wore riding britches and carried a short whip. A woman of courage and compassion, yet a very strong and demanding woman who could touch your life in a way you could not help from loving. This was Ammie Wilson.

Dudley M. Wilson
Special to Times Herald

PLANO — Last rites were held Wednesday for Dudley M. Wilson, 83, of Plano, who died Sunday from injuries received in an automobile accident.

He and his wife were en route to the Iowa State Fair when the accident occurred near Des Moines, Iowa. Mrs. Wilson is hospitalized in Dallas.

A native of Mansfield, Ohio, Mr. Wilson was graduated from the Colorado School of Mines. Formerly with Texas Power & Light Co., he had his own civil engineering construction company.

Survivors are his wife and a sister, Miss Florence Wilson of Oklahoma City.

Dallas Times Herald obituary for Dudley Wilson. Courtesy of the *Dallas Times Herald*.

Ammie Wilson

Eddie "Sarge" Stimpson Jr.

Ammie Wilson

Artwork created by Ammie

Artwork created by Ammie

Artwork created by Ammie

3

Epilogue: The Building of a Museum

Ammie Wilson with her show trophies at the 1970 dedication of the Ammie E. Wilson Junior High School. Courtesy of the *Plano Daily Post.*

This *Plano Star Courier* picture shows Marguerite Haggard loading items bought from the Dudley and Ammie Wilson estate sale in the spring of 1973. Mrs. Haggard was the chairman of the Collin County Historical Society and purchased the living room sofa and marble-top end pieces for the Plano Heritage Association; she later donated them to the museum. Courtesy of the *Plano Star Courier.*

Without any surviving children, Ammie Wilson's death signaled the end of an era for the Farrell-Wilson families and their home. Mary Alice had left half of the property to Buckner's Orphan Home in Dallas and half to the Juliette Fowler Home in St. Louis in the memory of her beloved grandson, George Hunter Lynch. However, in 1960 and 1961, each of the orphanages sold its share to Hunt Properties, who purchased it for the purpose of residential development. The Ammie E. Wilson Junior High School, located on land from the original farm, was dedicated in 1970. After Ammie's death in 1972, the estate was settled, but the home was unoccupied. During this period, the Plano Heritage Association formed out of a group of concerned citizens who wanted to save the farmstead from destruction. The Heritage Association raised $5,000 to match the same amount given by Hunt Properties in an effort to keep the property in their control.

In the spring of 1973, Mrs. Thelma Rice Sproles appealed to the City Council for monetary resources to build a historical museum fund, but her appeal was met with resistance. In April 1973, robbers stole antiques from the home; however, many items were recovered in June. Several Planoites,

Bill Hamm and Les Bonner of Hunt Properties present the deed of the Farrell-Wilson House to Joan Biggerstaff (left), president of the Plano Heritage Association, and Thelma Rice Sproles (center), founder of the organization, November 1975. Courtesy of the *Plano Star Courier*.

Farrell-Wilson House

Farrell-Wilson House

Aerial view of Farrell-Wilson farm, 1979

who had unwittingly bought the antique furniture, donated the objects back to the Heritage Association. Because of the theft, the decision was made to have live-in tenants as caretakers of the house. Bowman Middle School history teacher Mary DePeri and her husband, Frank, moved onto the property in the spring of 1974. The couple occupied the western portion of the second floor and kitchen until November 1981.

During the late 1970s and the early 1980s, the Plano Heritage Association continued its fundraising efforts in order to fully renovate the house and "create an on-site museum that represented the history of North Texas farming."

The first tour of the farmstead was in late 1974 and was an important "step toward making the landmark permanent." In 1975, the City of Plano bought the land for $10,608 an acre, Hunt Properties deeded the buildings to the Plano Heritage Association, and the City of Plano leased the four-acre site to the association.

As the Heritage Association continued in its efforts to form a museum, the house was included in a Bicentennial tour of historic homes in 1976 and a heritage day fundraiser to introduce the community to "a glimpse of farm life as it was in Plano before urbanization." This was the first time that the property had been given the mission of representing life in the Blackland Prairies. In 1977 the association presented Hunt Properties with an "Ammie" award in appreciation of their

This *Plano Star Courier* article from June 1975 shows Kathy Pritchett standing on the stairway in the Farrell-Wilson House, surrounded by objects donated to the Heritage Association. Courtesy of the *Plano Star Courier.*

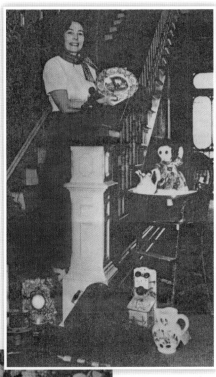

Frank and Mary DePeri lived on the second floor of the Farrell-Wilson House as property caretakers from 1974 to 1981. Courtesy of the *Plano Star Courier.*

First floor hallway

Family parlor

Dining room

Second floor hallway

Family bedroom

Girl's room

Potting shed

donation of the house and $5,000. In 1978, the house was added to the National Register of Historic Places.

In the 1980s, the house underwent a series of renovations to prepare for its opening as a full-time museum in 1986. It was repainted in its original 1890s color scheme. Other improvements to the house included foundation, chimney, and carpentry repair, firebox repainting, new wiring, climate control, an alarm system, fire suppression units, the decorative wooden trim stripped of the many layers of paint and brought back to its original oak finish, and the hanging of period wallpaper.

The overarching goal of the museum when it opened was to recreate agrarian life on the Blackland Prairies of Collin County from 1890 to 1940. Over time, the focus of the historic house shifted to concentrate on the period of 1890 through 1925. At the inception of the museum, it was believed that the location of the property in an urban area was an ideal setting for the understanding of "early electrification/mechanization" and for providing an

Curing shed

Root cellar

First Docent Council, 1986

example of the popular tastes, sociability, and family environment during this period. Interpretation by the museum remains consistent with these original goals.

Since the death of Ammie Wilson in 1972, the Farrell-Wilson house has been transformed from an old Victorian dwelling into an active historic house museum and farm. Hard work and determination of members of the Plano Heritage Association and many tireless supporters saved the property from destruction and raised the necessary funds to transform the house into a historical landmark. The continued efforts of staff, volunteers, supporters, and local historical organizations have allowed the museum to become a recognized institution within the community and state. It remains on the National Register of Historic Places, is a designated Texas Historic Site, and has been accredited by the American Alliance of Museums.

Above: The year 2011 marked the twenty-fifth anniversary of the Heritage Farmstead Museum being a full-time museum.

Right: Ammie Estelle Juhan Lynch Wilson montage

The farmstead is home to an array of livestock—sheep, donkeys, chickens, turkeys, guineas, and our friendly boer goat, Jack.

Buttermilk, the incredible milking cow, is one of the many hands-on educational components at the museum.

In honor of Ammie Wilson's contribution to the sheep business, the museum is still home to many "wooly" friends.

Outdoor cooking demonstrations are a favorite attraction for educational programs and special events.

A Collection of Watercolors of the Farrell-Wilson House

by Artist Nel Byrd

Formal parlor

Music room

Kitchen

Dining room

Family bedroom

Boy's room

Girl's room

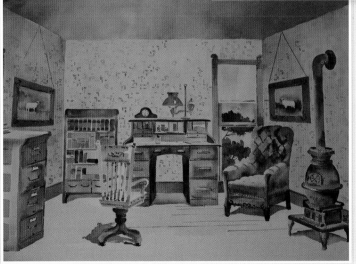

Office

Bibliography

Alabama, Deaths and Burials Index, 1881–1974 [database on-line]. Provo, UT, USA: Ancestry.com Operations, Inc., 2011. Accessed October 21, 2012, Woods Lynch.

"Ammie E. Wilson: Someone to Reckon With." N.d. Heritage Farmstead Collection.

"Ammie's Cupboard not Bare" Unknown paper. December 4, 1977. Heritage Farmstead Museum Collection.

"Another Statement." *Dallas Morning News*. October 1, 1887.

"Application for Official Texas Historical Marker Ammie Wilson House." Heritage Farmstead Collection.

"Architecture Across Space and Time." *Penn State University*. Accessed November 6, 2011. www.personal.psu.edu/ruo3/group.html.

"Association Organized." *Plano Daily Post*. June 10, 1973.

Barnes, Jeanne. "Plano Farmhouse on Tour." Unknown paper. December 8, 1974. Heritage Farmstead Museum Collection.

Blackwood, Sharon, letter to Florence Wilson, June 12, 1977. Heritage Farmstead Collection.

Boren, Winfred, oral history interview, August 15, 2000. Heritage Farmstead Collection.

Boyd and Heidrich Landscape Architects. "Landscape Development Design Development Presentation." Report to Plano Heritage Society, Plano, TX, 1984.

Campbell, Mozell, interview September 28, 1993. Heritage Farmstead Museum Collection.

Camphelli, Robin, note, September 28, 1993. Heritage Farmstead Collection.

Carter, Paul. "Miss Ammie As I Knew Her." January 1985. Heritage Farmstead Collection.

"Charles Henry Acquitted." *Dallas Morning News*. October 19, 1887.

Chopin, Kate. "The Role of Wife and Mother." *Loyola University New Orleans*. Accessed June 28, 2011. http://www.loyno.edu/~kchopin/new/women/motherhood.html.

"Citizens Internationally Known." PMP. July 4, 1976.

"The City." *Dallas Morning News*. April 19, 1887.

Clerk District Court, Collin County, Texas, Hunter Farrell vs. Walter B. Barkley et al., no. 16442.

Collin County District Records, 59th Judicial District of Texas, Mary Alice Farrell vs. Hunter T. Farrell no. 11751.

Collin County Probate Records. Last Will and Testament of Mary Alice Farrell Will, no. 4801.

"Council Hears Request from Plano Heritage." Unknown paper. Spring 1973. Heritage Farmstead Museum Collection.

Dallas County District Court Civil Case Papers No. 7169 (1889) M.A. Juhan vs. S.O. Juhan.

"David Crockett." *Texas State Library & Archives Commission.* Accessed October 16, 2011. https://www.tsl.state.tx.us/treasures/republic/alamo/crockett-01.html.

Davis, Maribelle. "Fire Boys," in *Plano, Texas: The Early Years*, 2nd ed. edited by Friends of the Plano Public Library, 363–371. Wolfe City, TX: Henington Publishing Co., 1996.

"Death of Mrs. Henry." *Dallas Morning News.* April 13, 1887.

District Court, 59th Judicial District, Collin County, TX, G.W. Ayer vs. H.T. Farrell, no. 11738.

District Court, County of Collin, State of Texas, E.M. Short vs. H.T. Farrell, no. 11461.

District Court, County of Collin, State of Texas, Ira Rudd vs. Hunter Farrell, no. 16638.

District Court, County of Collin, State of Texas, L. Stockton vs. H.T. Farrell, no. 11462.

District Court, County of Collin, State of Texas, Mrs. Corrie B. Farrell vs. Jess Farrell et al.

District Court, County of Collin, State of Texas, O.B. Freeman vs. Farrell, no. 15331.

District Court, County of Collin, State of Texas, Truett, Abernathy, and Wolford vs. Hunter T. Farrell, no. 15591.

District Court of Collin County, TX, Jack Donathan vs. H.T. Farrell, no. 11721.

District Court of Midland County, Texas. February Term, 1915. No. 1021.

District Court of Midland County, Texas. September Term A.D. 1914 No. 1021, W.W. Lynch vs. Ammie Lynch.

"Dudley Wilson Services Held." *Unknown newspaper*, n.d. Heritage Farmstead Collection.

"Early Settler: William Foreman." *Plano Daily Post* (Plano, TX), August 12, 1973.

"Early Social Life Busy." *Plano Daily Post.* December 8, 1973.

Enstam, Elizabeth York. "Women and the Law." *Texas Historical Association.* Accessed July 6, 2011. http://www.tshaonline.org/handbook/online/articles/jsw02.

Farrell, Mrs. Tom, interview, May 18, 1977. Heritage Farmstead Collection.

Francell, Beth, N.E.H. Grant Proposal, June 25, 1984. Heritage Farmstead Museum Collection.

"Free Hand Shooting." *Dallas Morning News.* September 30, 1887.

Hall, Captain Roy F. "Mis Ammie Wilson Exhibits Sheep." *McKinney Daily Courier Gazette.* October 20, 1952.

Hardison, Jane. *Times Herald.*

Harrell, Peggy. *Plano Fire Rescue: 125 Years of Serving.* Evansville, IN: M.T. Publishing Co., Inc., 2011.

Harrington, Ann, and Jean Elizabeth, oral history interview, July 12, 2000.

"Heard and Overheard." *Dallas Morning News.* December 5, 1982.

"The Henry Killing Case." *Dallas Morning News.* April 15, 1887.

"The Heritage Farmstead Museum's History." *Heritage Farmstead Museum.*

http://www.heritagefarmstead.org/history.htm (accessed October 30, 2011).

"Heritage House Events Plans for Funds." PMP. December 1977.

"Heritage Plans Celebration." *Plano Morning Press*. September 4, 1977.

"Hunter Lynch of Plano Claimed by Grim Reaper: Died in Dallas Hospital." Newspaper clipping of unknown origin, n.d. Heritage Farmstead Museum Collection.

Index of Vital Records for Alabama: Deaths, 1908–1959. Montgomery, AL: State of Alabama Center for Health Statistics, Record Services Division. Woods Lynch.

Kelly, Joan B. "The Determination of Child Custody." *The Future of Children* 4, no. 1 (1994): 121–142.

"Long-time resident recalls Plano's early days." *Plano Star Courier*. September 28, 1986.

Lynch, Johnny, interview by Peggy Riddle transcript, n.d. Dallas Historical Society.

Lynch, Woods, letter to Hunter Lynch, March 11, 1914. Heritage Farmstead Collection.

Lynch, Woods, letter to Mary Alice Farrell, March 14, 1914. Heritage Farmstead Collection.

"The Many Moods of Christmas." *Plano Star Courier*. December 8, 1974.

McKnight, Joseph W. "Texas Community Property Law: Conservative Attitudes, Reluctant Change." *Law and Contemporary Problems* 71, no. 2 (1993): 71–98. Accessed July 6, 2011. www.jstor.org.

McLaurin, Banks, Jr. "Morrison Family." 1995.

Midland County Historical Society. "The Pioneer History of Midland County, Texas: 1880–1926." Dallas: Taylor, 1984.

Milner, Clyde A., II, Carol A. O'Connor, and Martha A. Sandweiss. *The Oxford History of the American West*. New York: Oxford University Press, 1994.

"Mrs. Ammie E. Wilson: She Knows How to Show Sheep." *Sheep and Goat Raiser: The Ranchman's Magazine*. January 1952.

National Archives. Year: *1860*; Census Place: *Charlotte, Virginia*; Roll: *M653_1340*; Page: *238*; Image: *244*; Family History Library Film: *805340*.

National Archives. Year: *1860*; Census Place: *Precinct 9, Collin, Texas*; Roll: *M653_1291*; Page: *101*; Image: *211*; Family History Library Film: *805291*.

National Archives. Year: *1870*; Census Place: *Bacon, Charlotte, Virginia*; Roll: *M593_1640*; Page: *31B*; Image: *67*; Family History Library Film: *553139*.

National Archives. Year: *1880*; Census Place: *Precinct 5, Collin, Texas*; Roll: *1296*; Page: *209D*; Enumeration District: *025;* Family History Film: *1255296*.

National Archives. Year: *1900*; Census Place: *Justice Precinct 1, Johnson, Texas*; Roll: *1649*; Page: *17B*; Enumeration District: *56*; FHL microfilm: *1241649*.

National Archives. Year: *1900*; Census Place: *Justice Precinct 5, Collin, Texas*; Roll: *1621*; Page: *20B*; Enumeration District: *16*; FHL microfilm: *1241621*.

National Archives. Year: *1910*; Census Place: *Midland, Midland, Texas*; Roll: *T624_1576*;

Page: *22A*; Enumeration District: *0164*; Image: *645*; FHL microfilm: *1375589.*

National Archives. Year: *1930*; Census Place: *Mineral Wells, Palo Pinto, Texas*; Roll: *2382*; Page: *11A*; Enumeration District: *10*; Image: *311.0*; FHL microfilm: *2342116.* Ammie Wilson.

National Archives. Year: *1940*; Census Place: *Collin, Texas*; Roll: *T627_4009*; Page: *10A*; Enumeration District: *43-32.*

Orr, Richard. "Day by Day on the Farm." *Chicago Daily Tribune.* November 30, 1955.

Passenger Lists of Vessels Arriving at New Orleans, Louisiana, 1903–1945; Series: *T905*; Roll: *66.* Dudley Moores Wilson.

"Plano." *Texas Historical Association.* Accessed September 18, 2011 http://www.texasalmanac.com/texas-towns/plano.

"Plano, Texas." *U.S. Census Bureau.* Accessed October 21, 2012. http://quickfacts.census.gov/qfd/states/48/4858016.html.

"Plano Boom Town." *Dallas Morning News.* April 4, 1976.

"Plano Breeder Gets Chicago's Top Sheep Prize." *Chicago Times Herald.* December 4, 1952.

"Plano Pickups." Dallas Morning News. 5 January 1887.

Plano Star Courier. May 14, 1975.

"Plano Timeline." Plano.gov. Last modified February 17, 2011. http://www.plano.gov/Site CollectionDocuments/Plano/Library/glhta/planotimeline.pdf.

Pratt, Box, Henderson Architects. "Farrell-Wilson Farm Historic Structure Report." Report to Heritage Farmstead Museum, Plano, TX, 1980.

Probate, Collin County No. 2911, Estate of Geo Hunter Lynch year–1918 minor.

"Prominent Mason Who Died Sunday at Camp Sheridan." *Dallas Morning News.* Heritage Farmstead Collection, n.d.

Randles, E.A., interview, April 12, 1985. Heritage Farmstead Museum Collection.

"Remembering Ammie Wilson." *Plano Star Courier.* May 12, 2000.

"Restoration earns firm first 'Ammie.'" *Dallas Times Herald.* November 27, 1977.

Rice, Thelma, letter to charter members, May 28, 1975. Heritage Farmstead Museum Collection.

Riddle, Peggy, "Interview with Mrs. Lynch," n.d. Heritage Farmstead Museum Collection.

"The Role of Wife and Mother." *Loyola University.* Accessed June 28, 2011. http://www.loyno.edu/~kchopin/new/women/motherhood.html.

Rowe, Meredith. "Plano's growth continues as city undergoes changes." *Plano Star Courier* (Plano, TX), July 2, 2000.

Sanders, Juanita, interview by Heritage Farmstead Museum staff member, April 3, 1985.

"Saturday's Tragedy." *Dallas Morning News.* April 19, 1887.

Schell, Shirley, and Francis B. Wells. "Plano, TX." *Texas State Historical Association.*

Accessed July 31, 2011. http://www.tshaonline.org/handbook/online/articles/hdp04.

17th District of Tarrant County, Texas, C.V. Fox vs. H.T. Farrell, no. 11239-a.

"72-Year-Old 'Miss Ammie' Raises Blue Ribbon Sheep." Unknown paper, unknown date. Heritage Farmstead Museum Collection.

Shaw, Susan M.. and Janet Lee. *Women's Voices Feminist Visions: Classic and Contemporary Readings*, 3rd ed. St. Louis: McGraw Hill, 2007.

State of Alabama. *Index of Vital Records for Alabama: Deaths, 1908–1959*. Montgomery, AL: State of Alabama Center for Health Statistics, Record Services Division. www.ancestry.com (accessed August 2011).

State of Texas, County of Collin. Marriage Record of Dr. W.W. Lynch and Miss Ammie E. Juhan. November 27, 1901.

State of Texas, County of Collin County, Marriage Record, 476.

State of Texas To-wit, Collin County. Marriage Record H.T. Farrell to Alice Lanham. March 5, 1889.

"A Terrible Tragedy." *Dallas Morning News*. April 10, 1887.

"Texas Architecture: A Visual History." *University of Texas*. Accessed November 6, 2011. http://www.lib.utexas.edu/exhibits/txarch/victorian.html.

Texas State Department of Health, Bureau of Vital Statistics. Standard Certificate of Death. Ammie Wilson.

Texas State Department of Health, Bureau of Vital Statistics. Standard Certificate of Death. 1603. George Hunter Lynch.

Texas State Department of Health, Bureau of Vital Statistics. Standard Certificate of Death. 36076. Mary Alice Farrell.

Texas State Department of Health, Bureau of Vital Statistics. Standard Certificate of Death. 53896. Hunter Thomas Farrell.

Tolney, Stewart E. "The African American 'Great Migration' and Beyond." *Annual Review of Sociology* 29 (2003): 209–232.

US, World War I Draft Registration Cards, 1917–1918, Registration State: *Texas*; Registration County: *Dallas*; Roll: *1953182*; Draft Board: *3*. Dudley Moores Wilson.

Wade, Harry E. "Peter's Colony." *Handbook of Texas Online*. Accessed July 25, 2011. http://www.tshaonline.org/handbook/online/articles/uep02.

Wampler, Mack. "Ammie Wilson's Back: 'Yellow Rose of Texas' Returns." Unknown newspaper, unknown date. Heritage Farmstead Museum Collection.

Whitehead, Nelda. "Museum Nearer to Reality: Combined Efforts Give Push to Dream." Unknown paper, unknown date. Heritage Farmstead Museum Collection.

Whitehead, Nelda. "PHA Antiques Found" Unknown paper. June 14, 1974. Heritage Farmstead Museum Collection.

"Wife of Early Real Estate Man Succumbs." *Dallas Morning News*. July 14, 1941.

Wilson, Ammie, letter to Ammir R. Eldon, September 13, 1961. Heritage Farmstead Museum Collection.

Wilson, Ammie, letter to Johnny Lynch, June 9, 1966: Heritage Farmstead Museum Collection.

Wilson, Florence, letter to Johnny Lynch, June 9, 1966. Heritage Farmstead Museum Collection.

Wilson, Florence O., "Biography of Dudley Moores Wilson," Heritage Farmstead Museum Collection, August 10, 1977.

"Wilson House Earns Honor." *Plano Daily Star-Courier*. April 9, 1978.

"Woods Lynch Obituary." *Dallas Morning News*. N.d. Heritage Farmstead Museum Collection.

❅ About the Authors ❅

Hillary Kidd graduated from the University of Delaware with a degree in Art Conservation, Collections Care, and a minor in American Material Culture. She received her Master of Liberal Arts degree in Museum Studies from Harvard University. Before returning home to Texas, she worked at the Museum of Fine Arts, Boston, as a Textile Collections Care Specialist and then as a Curatorial Assistant in the Textile and Fashion Arts Department. She is currently the Curator of Collections and Exhibitions at the Heritage Farmstead Museum.

Jessica Bell graduated from the University of Tulsa in 2008 with a major in history and minor in religion. She went on to attend the University of Oklahoma and graduated with a Master of Arts degree in Museum Studies in 2011. She has volunteered at the Heritage Farmstead Museum since 2011 and served as the curatorial assistant at the International Bowling Museum and Hall of Fame. She is currently continuing her studies at the University of Texas at Dallas in their Humanities PhD program.